A CHRISTMAS CAROL

By Charles Dickens
Dramatized by Martha B. King

Dramatic Publishing Company
Woodstock, Illinois • Australia • New Zealand • South Africa

*** NOTICE ***

IMPORTANT BILLING AND CREDIT REQUIREMENTS

All producers of the play *must* give credit to the author of the play in all programs distributed in connection with performances of the play and in all instances in which the title of the play appears for purposes of advertising, publicizing or otherwise exploiting the play and/or a production. The name of the author *must* also appear on a separate line, on which no other name appears, immediately following the title, and *must* appear in size of type not less than fifty percent (50%) the size of the title type. Biographical information on the author, if included in the playbook, may be used in all programs. *In all programs this notice must appear:*

"Produced by special arrangement with
THE DRAMATIC PUBLISHING COMPANY, INC., of Woodstock, Illinois."

ORIGINAL PRODUCTION CREDIT

This dramatization of A CHRISTMAS CAROL was first produced on December 26, 1939, by the JACK AND JILL PLAYERS of Chicago, Illinois, under the direction of Miss Marie Agnes Foley. A later production of this play was given by the Portland, OREGON CIVIC THEATRE.

SCENE SYNOPSIS
ACT ONE
Scene 1. The Cratchit kitchen

Scene 2. Scrooge's office

ACT TWO
Scene 1. The schoolroom—of the past

Scene 2. Fezziwig's ball—of the past

Scene 3. The Cratchit kitchen—of the past

ACT THREE
Scene 1. A graveyard—of the future

Scene 2. The Cratchit kitchen—of the future

Scene 3. Scrooge's office—the real present

Scene 4. The Cratchit kitchen

PRODUCTION NOTES

The full stage is designed for the Cratchit kitchen with only a few pieces of furniture. A movable set consisting of a low back wall and two wings or a curtain may be used center stage for Scrooge's office, the schoolroom, the ball, and the graveyard.

Scrooge and the ghost stand on ladders behind the movable set, giving the appearance of viewing the action from the air. Scene changes are effected by blackouts, lights and sound effects without lowering the main curtain. Curtain drops at end of acts only.

(Property List included page 57.)

Play Script Design: Randy Blevins, jrbdesign

CAST OF CHARACTERS

ACT ONE

BOB CRATCHIT
MRS. CRATCHIT
THE CRATCHIT CHILDREN
      TINY TIM, AGE 10
      PETER, AGE 17
      BELINDA, AGE 15
      MARTHA, AGE 18
      EDWARD, AGE 8
      ELIZABETH, AGE 7
EBENEZER SCROOGE
FRED, SCROOGE'S NEPHEW
MAN
MARLEY'S GHOST
THE GHOST OF CHRISTMAS PAST

ACT TWO

THE GHOST OF CHRISTMAS PRESENT
EBENEZER SCROOGE
EBENEZER, AS A YOUNG BOY
FAN, HIS LITTLE SISTER
SCHOOLBOYS
      GEORGE
      ROB
      FRED
MR. FEZZIWIG
MRS. FEZZIWIG
EBENEZER, APPRENTICE
DICK, FELLOW APPRENTICE
CHARLOTTE
FIDDLER
DANCERS
THE CRATCHIT FAMILY

ACT THREE

THE GHOST OF CHRISTMAS FUTURE
EBENEZER SCROOGE
JOE, A FENCE FOR STOLEN GOODS
A CHARWOMAN
A LAUNDRESS
AN UNDERTAKER'S MAN
THE CRATCHIT FAMILY
MAN

A Christmas Carol
by Charles Dickens
Dramatized by Martha B. King

ACT ONE
SCENE ONE

(The Cratchit kitchen, cheerful and hearty like the Cratchits, but scantily furnished. It is early morning. The room is cold. Mrs. Cratchit hurries in to start the fire for breakfast. Peter follows.)

PETER: Wait, Mother, I'm coming. I'll lay the fire. *(He snatches sticks from box.)*

MRS. C: *(Lovingly)* Oh, Peter. I told you to get some extra sleep. You worked so late last night.

PETER: Do you think I could sleep and let my mother lay the fire?

MRS. C: You're a dear. But I declare, I couldn't sleep a wink myself.

PETER: Is Tiny Tim worse?

MRS. C: No, Tim's the same as usual. It's your father that's on my mind. Peter, it's the day before Christmas and Mr. Scrooge still hasn't told your father he could take the holiday off.

PETER: Nobody can refuse to give Christmas Day.

MRS. C: Nobody with a heart. Oh, it's a dreadful thing to say of any man, but that Scrooge has a piece of ice where a heart should be.

PETER: I think I'll go and talk to him myself.

MRS. C: *(Horrified)* Peter! Your father wouldn't hear of it.

PETER: Don't tell him. He's coming now.

BOB: *(Enters; puts an arm around Mrs. C. and warms hands at the stove)* Good morning, my dear.

(Mrs. C. pats his face lovingly.)

PETER: 'Morning, Father.

BOB: Good morning, son. It's a raw, cold morning, it is.

MRS. C: Warm yourself by the fire, dear. Your breakfast will be ready in a minute.

BOB: I don't seem to feel hungry this morning.

MRS. C: Now you just sit down and compose yourself. You can't go to work without eating your breakfast—hungry or no hungry.

BOB: I looked in at Tiny Tim as I came down.

PETER: How is he this morning?

BOB: Cheerful, as always.

MRS. C: I do wish he'd get some color in his cheeks again.

PETER: I'll take him outdoors today, Mother.

BOB: *(Clearing throat)* Hm... Tim wanted me to ask you if he could come down for breakfast with me.

MRS. C: Oh, no, he mustn't. He'll catch his death of cold.

BOB: *(Disappointed)* Yes. Yes, that's what I told him.

MRS. C: After it gets warmer in here—

PETER: I could carry him down, Mother, and bring a blanket to wrap him in.

BOB: *(Eagerly)* That would be all right, wouldn't it, Mother?

MRS. C: *(Putting arm around his neck)* You do hate to go off without talking to Tim, don't you?

BOB: It's a long time before I get home at night.

MRS. C: Bless you. Of course it is. And Tim will be sorry all day if he doesn't see you. *(Peter dashes out. Mrs. C. calls.)* Peter, bring the blanket from my bed.

BOB: Well, tomorrow's Christmas.

MRS. C: Doesn't seem any time since last Christmas, does it?

BOB: I haven't bought anything for the children.

MRS. C: Mercy. They don't want a lot of things. Not when we have each other. And don't forget that Martha's coming.

BOB: It will be nice to have our Martha home.

MRS. C: She might even come tonight.

BOB: Mother, do you have enough money to buy what you need for dinner tomorrow?

MRS. C: I'll manage.

BOB: I'm sure you haven't much money left.

MRS. C: Now you just leave everything to me, Bob Cratchit. What we have for dinner is going to be a surprise.

BOB: I'm a mighty poor husband to you, I am.

MRS. C: Shame on you. Nobody ever had a better husband.

BOB: Fifteen bob a week! It's not enough to support a family decently.

MRS. C: And whose fault is that? You ought to be getting thirty for the work you do. Bob, why don't you ask Mr. Scrooge for a raise?

BOB: Ask Scrooge? He'd sooner see me dead than give me a shilling more. I'll be fortunate if he lets me take tomorrow off without taking something off my salary.

MRS. C: He couldn't be so mean. Bob, couldn't you tell him about Tiny Tim?

BOB: He wouldn't listen.

MRS. C: If he could only see him once.

BOB: I wouldn't let him lay eyes on the child. We'll manage.

MRS. C: And yet—we must get Tim to the doctor again. And he ought to be having special food. Bob, if he doesn't—if he doesn't—we may not have him. *(She starts to cry.)*

BOB: There now, don't cry. Tears aren't going to help matters. Here. *(Hands her his handkerchief)* Quick.

EDWARD and ELIZABETH: *(Off)* Make way. Make way for his highness. *(They come marching on.)* Make way. Make way for his highness.

BELINDA: *(Entering)* Make way for Tiny Tim.

(There are shouts of laughter as Peter follows, carrying Tiny Tim. Bob leaps up and bows low.)

BOB: Where does it please his highness to sit this morning?

TIM: *(Pointing majestically)* There. On the golden throne.

BOB: Spread out the fur robes for his highness.

(The younger children spread out the blankets in the chair. Peter deposits Tim. They all wrap him up.)

TIM: *(Grandly, still playing the game)* Thank you one and all.

BOB: Comfortable now? *(He gives Tim a hug.)*

MRS. C: Be sure the blanket's wrapped around his feet. He mustn't catch cold.

BOB: All warm?

TIM: Yes, thank you.

MRS. C: All right, children. Sit down in your places.

BELINDA: I'll carry the porridge bowls, Mother.

TIM: *(Leaning toward Bob and whispering in a voice he intends to have overheard)* You must have known just the right words to say to her. I was afraid she wouldn't let me come down. *(They look at Mrs. C and grin.)*

BOB: *(Archly)* If you speak to her kindly, she's a very reasonable woman.

MRS. C: Get along with you both. You'd think I was first cousin to Scrooge to hear you talk.

PETER: Mother, how can you say such a thing?

BELINDA: I don't even like to hear his name.

EDWARD and ELIZABETH: Neither do I.

BOB: *(Cheerfully)* What if you had to look at him every day the way I do?

BELINDA: Poor Father.

BOB: Well, if I don't hurry I won't have a chance to see him any more. *(Bob leaves the table.)*

TIM: Tomorrow you won't have to see him at all.

BOB: I hope not.

BELINDA: Hope not?

PETER: Father, you're going to stay at home tomorrow!

TIM: It's Christmas Day.

BOB: I know it... I know it.

TIM: You said you would play with me all day tomorrow.

BOB: I want to. I want to.

PETER: We're all going to slide on Cornhill Road.

BELINDA: And we're going to play Blindman's Buff and Forfeits.

EDWARD: Martha's going to be here.

TIM: And you promised to take me to church with you.

BELINDA: It won't be like Christmas at all if you don't stay at home.

BOB: Now, now. I'm going to do the very best I can. If old Scrooge isn't in too sour a mood.

MRS. C: Darling, tell Mr. Scrooge that you're going to stay at home.

BELINDA: I hope something terrible happens to him if he doesn't let you.

PETER: He can't refuse. He can't do it.

TIM: Please, Father. Tell him you have to stay at home.

BOB: I'll tell him all right... but I must hurry now. Who's going to meet me at the corner tonight?

TIM: I am. If somebody will take me.

ALL: I'll take you.

BOB: Good. I'll be watching for you.

TIM: Will you carry me on your back?

BOB: I'm the most spirited blood horse in town. Watch me prance. *(He prances and shouts good-bye.)*

CHILDREN: Good-bye. Good-bye.

MRS. C: Bob Cratchit, you've forgotten your scarf. Come back here.

BELINDA: I'll get it for you, Father. *(Takes it from a chair and puts it around his neck.)*

BOB: I could keep warm just thinking about my fine family.

MRS. C: Just the same, this scarf will come in handy.

BOB: I'm off. Good-bye.

MRS. C: Be sure to keep the fire going in your work room.

BOB: *(Off)* Good-bye.

TIM: He must stay at home tomorrow.

MRS. C: Now, we won't think about it any more. We'll just pray that the good Lord will soften Mr. Scrooge's heart.

TIM: Maybe we could do more than that.

BELINDA: What could we do?

TIM: *(Motions to others to gather around—all except his mother)* You go away, Mother.

MRS. C: Indeed, you'll have no secrets from me. Out with it.

TIM: Well, maybe Mr. Scrooge has forgotten that it's Christmas. And Father doesn't like to mention things to him.

BELINDA: Do you mean we ought to tell him?

TIM: We could go and sing carols to him.

MRS. C: Tim!

TIM: I'm not afraid to go.

MRS. C: You'll not set foot in that counting house. My, but your father would be angry.

PETER: I think Tim's right, Mother. Mr. Scrooge might listen to us.

MRS. C: He never would. Not in the whole wide world.

PETER: We can try, can't we, Tim? I'll carry you all the way on my shoulder.

EDWARD: I'll carry your crutch.

BELINDA: Well, I don't exactly like to go—but if one of us goes we'd better all go.

MRS. C: Oh, children. I oughtn't to let you do it.

TIM: If it helps father to stay at home, you'll like it, won't you?

MRS. C: Yes, darling.

BELINDA: What are we going to sing, Tim?

TIM: *(Sings)* GOD REST YOU MERRY GENTLEMEN

ALL: *(Join singing)* LET NOTHING YOU DISMAY

(The singing continues after the scene is out of sight, and while the unit set is put into position.)

ACT ONE
SCENE TWO

(Scrooge's office. Scrooge is sitting at a high desk. There is a coal box beside him and one extra chair. Bob works in another room. As the scene opens, he enters with a shovel in his hand. Scrooge has just closed the door tightly to shut out the sound of carols.)

BOB: *(Self-consciously)* Weather seems to be getting colder.

SCROOGE: *(Without looking up)* Cold? Humbug. It doesn't feel cold to me. *(Suddenly sees Bob taking coal)* What are you doing with that shovel?

BOB: I thought I'd put another coal on my fire... if it's quite all right.

SCROOGE: It isn't all right. What do you expect me to do? Buy enough coal to heat the whole outdoors?

BOB: No, sir. But my fire's almost out. My hand's so cold I can hardly write.

SCROOGE: Blow on it.

(Bob tries to blow on his frozen hands. The sound of carols grows louder. Scrooge opens the door.)

SCROOGE: Keep quiet out there. *(The music stops. Scrooge returns to desk.)* Police ought to shut those people up. Singing around in the streets as if they had no proper business. *(Sees Bob still standing)* Well, what are you standing there for? It isn't closing time by half an hour.

BOB: About tomorrow, sir.

SCROOGE: What about tomorrow?

BOB: It's Christmas time, sir.

SCROOGE: A clerk with fifteen shillings a week and a wife and family talking about Christmas.

BOB: But my children are counting on –

SCROOGE: I'm not interested in hearing about your children. And if you stand about talking much longer, we'll be obliged to part company.

BOB: Yes, sir. *(Hurries off.)*

(There is a loud knocking on the door.)

SCROOGE: Answer that door. I don't want to see anybody!

(Bob opens the door. A man is there.)

MAN: Scrooge and Marley's, I believe? *(He sees Scrooge and brushes past Bob with a nod.)* Oh... thank you. Have I the pleasure of addressing Mr. Scrooge or Mr. Marley?

SCROOGE: Mr. Marley has been dead these seven years.

MAN: Indeed!

SCROOGE: He died seven years ago this very night.

MAN: Very sad. Very sad. Well, I have no doubt his generosity is well represented in his surviving partner. My credentials, sir. *(Hands papers to Scrooge who hands them right back.)* At this festive season of the year, Mr. Scrooge, we all want to make some slight provision for the poor and destitute. *(He picks up a pen and holds it toward Scrooge.)* Many thousands are in want of common necessities; hundreds of thousands are in want of common comforts.

SCROOGE: Are there no prisons?

MAN: Plenty of prisons. *(Lays down pen.)*

SCROOGE: What about the Union workhouses? Are they still in operation?

MAN: They are. I wish I could say they were not.

SCROOGE: The treadmill and the Poor Law. Are they still effective?

MAN: I'm sorry to say they are.

SCROOGE: Oh. I was afraid from what you said at first that something had stopped them in their useful work.

MAN: They scarcely furnish Christian cheer for mind and body. *(He makes a fresh start.)* Now, Mr. Scrooge, a few of us are trying to raise a fund to buy meat and drink for the poor. We choose this time because it is the time when want is felt most keenly. What shall I put you down for?

SCROOGE: Nothing.

MAN: I see. You wish to give money but to keep your name hidden.

SCROOGE: I wish to be left alone. I don't make myself merry at Christmas and I can't afford to make a lot of idle people merry. I pay taxes to support the prisons and poor houses. They cost enough. Those who are badly off must go there.

MAN: Many would rather die than go there.

SCROOGE: If they would rather die, they had better do it and decrease the surplus population. Besides, this has nothing to do with my business.

MAN: You ought to make it your business. You ought to help your fellow man.

SCROOGE: It's enough for a man to understand his own business and not interfere with other people's. Mine occupies me constantly. Good afternoon.

MAN: If Mr. Marley felt as you do, I fear his ghost is not resting in peace. Good afternoon. *(As he opens the door, Scrooge's nephew, Fred, enters in high spirits.)*

FRED: Merry Christmas, sir.

MAN: Merry Christmas to you, sir. *(He leaves.)*

SCROOGE: *(Turns on his stool in fury)* What's all this shouting about? *(He sees Fred and turns back to his desk, pretending to be very busy.)*

FRED: A merry Christmas to you, Uncle. God save you.

SCROOGE: Bah. Humbug.

FRED: Christmas a humbug, Uncle? You don't mean that, I'm sure.

SCROOGE: I do. Merry Christmas. What right have you to be merry? What reason have you to be merry? You're poor enough.

FRED: Come then. What right have you to be dismal? You're rich enough.

SCROOGE: Bah. Humbug.

FRED: Don't be cross, Uncle.

SCROOGE: What else can I be when I live in such a world of fools as this? Merry Christmas. Out upon Merry Christmas. What's Christmas time to you but a time for paying bills without money? A time for finding yourself a year older and not an hour richer. If I could work my will, every idiot who goes about with Merry Christmas on his lips should be boiled with his own pudding.

FRED: Uncle!

SCROOGE: Yes, and buried with a stake of holly through his heart.

FRED: Oh, really, Uncle.

SCROOGE: Oh, really, Nephew. Keep Christmas in your own way and let me keep it in mine.

FRED: Keep it! But you don't keep it.

SCROOGE: Let me leave it alone then. Much good may it do you. Much good it has ever done you.

FRED: Uncle, I believe it has done me good. It's the only time I know of when men and women seem to open their shut-up hearts freely... and though it has never put a scrap of gold or silver in my pocket, I believe it has done me good, and will do me good, and I say, GOD BLESS IT.

(Bob has appeared at the doorway of his work-room in time to

hear this speech.)

BOB: *(Claps)* Splendid, sir. Splendid.

(Scrooge leaps up. Bob hurries off.)

SCROOGE: Another sound from you, and you'll keep your Christmas by losing your situation. *(He turns to Fred.)* You're quite a powerful speaker, sir. I wonder you don't go into Parliament.

FRED: Don't be angry, Uncle. Come dine with us tomorrow.

SCROOGE: I'll have dinner with the devil first.

FRED: But why? Why?

SCROOGE: Why did you get married?

FRED: Because I fell in love.

SCROOGE: Because you fell in love. Good afternoon.

FRED: But you never came to see me before I married. Why use it as an excuse for not coming now?

SCROOGE: Good afternoon.

FRED: I want nothing from you. I ask nothing of you. Why can't we be friends?

SCROOGE: Good afternoon.

FRED: I am sorry with all my heart to find you so resolute.

SCROOGE: Good afternoon.

FRED: We never had any quarrels to which I have been a party.

SCROOGE: Good afternoon.

FRED: Well, I have made this trial in homage to Christmas, and I'll keep my Christmas humor to the last. So, a Merry Christmas to you, Uncle. *(Starts out)*

SCROOGE: Good afternoon.

FRED: *(Putting his head back in the door)* And a Happy New Year.

(Scrooge sits at his desk and writes furiously. The Cratchit children peek in. Carefully they put Tiny Tim on the floor and give him his crutch. They gesticulate to each other. Then Tim holds up his hand and they start to sing.)

CHILDREN: *(Sing)* GOD REST YOU MERRY GENTLEMEN
            LET NOTHING YOU DISMAY

SCROOGE: Who let you in here?

TIM: How do you do, Mr. Scrooge.

SCROOGE: Get out of here.

TIM: We've come to sing you some carols.

SCROOGE: Get out of here, I say.

TIM: It's Christmas time.

(Scrooge reaches for a coal. Peter grabs Tim and they all disappear. Scrooge throws the coal at the door.)

BOB: *(Hurrying in)* What is it, sir?

SCROOGE: Just let me lay hands on those young ruffians.

BOB: Who were they, sir?

SCROOGE: Brats. Christmas. Bah. Humbug. *(Sits down and looks at watch.)* Well, I suppose you might as well go. It's five minutes past time. Get along.

BOB: Yes, sir.

SCROOGE: Well, what are you waiting for?

BOB: About tomorrow, sir.

SCROOGE: Don't tell me it's Christmas or I'll... I'll...

BOB: Yes, sir. No, sir. I'll be taking tomorrow off... if it's quite convenient.

SCROOGE: It isn't convenient. And it's not fair. If I deduct something from your salary, you'll think you are being ill used, I'll be bound.

BOB: My salary is not enough to support my family now, sir.

SCROOGE: So you think you'll take tomorrow off.

BOB: It's only once a year, sir.

SCROOGE: A poor excuse for picking a man's pockets every twenty-fifth of December. I suppose you want the whole day.

BOB: Yes, sir.

SCROOGE: All right. If you came tomorrow, you wouldn't do any work. You'd do nothing but prate about Christmas all the time. Take the day – but be here all the earlier the next morning.

BOB: Very well, sir... I hope you have a pleasant day, sir. *(Bob goes out.)*

(Scrooge turns to his desk. Outside a carol is heard. He goes to the door and locks it. Then he returns to double lock it. It is dark. He sits on the stool at his desk. A bell begins to toll, then stops. There is a loud clanking noise. Scrooge listens... saying "humbug" at intervals. Suddenly the locked door opens, and Marley's ghost appears.)

SCROOGE: *(Rubs his eyes)* Humbug, I say. That door is locked. *(The ghost clanks to a stop.)* Well... what do you want of me?

MARLEY'S GHOST: Much.

SCROOGE: Who are you?

MARLEY'S GHOST: Ask me who I was.

SCROOGE: Who were you then?

MARLEY'S GHOST: In life I was your partner, Jacob Marley.

SCROOGE: Jacob Marley! What do you want of me?

MARLEY'S GHOST: Much.

SCROOGE: Can you... can you sit down? *(He points to a chair, gulping a little.)*

MARLEY'S GHOST: I can.

SCROOGE: Do it then.

MARLEY'S GHOST: *(Sits down)* You don't believe in me?

SCROOGE: I don't.

MARLEY'S GHOST: You can see me, can't you?

SCROOGE: I think I can.

MARLEY'S GHOST: Why do you doubt your own senses?

SCROOGE: Because a little thing affects my senses... a slight disorder of the stomach... a bit of undigested beef, a blot of mustard, a crumb of cheese, a fragment of an underdone potato. There's more of gravy than of the grave about you, whatever you are. Ha... ha.

(The ghost stares with fixed eyes. Scrooge, who isn't accustomed to cracking jokes, laughs hard, then, terrified by the ghostly stare, laughs mirthlessly. The final "ha... ha" is almost whispered. Then he tries to disprove his senses another way. He holds up a toothpick.)

SCROOGE: You see this toothpick?

MARLEY'S GHOST: I do.

SCROOGE: You aren't looking at it.

MARLEY'S GHOST: But I see it.

SCROOGE: Well, if I swallow this toothpick, I'll have such indigestion I'll be persecuted by a whole legion of goblins... all my own creation. Humbug, I tell you. Humbug.

(The ghost raises a frightful cry and shakes his chains. Scrooge falls onto his chair and tries not to swoon. The ghost unties the bandage from his chin and lets his mouth drop open. Scrooge falls on his knees.)

SCROOGE: Mercy... oh, mercy!

(The ghost ties up his chin again.)

MARLEY'S GHOST: Do you believe in me or not?

SCROOGE: I do. I must. But why do spirits walk on earth? And why do they come to me?

MARLEY'S GHOST: It is required of every man that the spirit in him should walk abroad among his fellow men and travel far and wide. If that spirit does not go out in life, it is condemned to do so after death. It is doomed to wander through the world... oh, woe is me. *(He wails dismally.)*

SCROOGE: You are chained; tell me why.

MARLEY'S GHOST: I wear the chain I forged in life. I made it link by link.

SCROOGE: Who put it on you?

MARLEY'S GHOST: I girded it on of my own free will. Is its pattern strange to you?

SCROOGE: I've never seen anything like it before.

MARLEY'S GHOST: That's strange. You wear a chain yourself. *(Scrooge looks anxiously about.)* It was as heavy and as long as this seven Christmas Eve's ago. You've made it longer since.

SCROOGE: Oh, Jacob, please don't talk like this. Say something to comfort me.

MARLEY'S GHOST: I have no comfort for you.

SCROOGE: But you were always a good man of business, Jacob.

MARLEY'S GHOST: Mankind was my business. I did nothing to help my fellow man... Oh, woe is me. *(He wails and holds his chain.)*

SCROOGE: Is something hurting you?

MARLEY'S GHOST: I suffer most at Christmas time. Oh, why did I walk through the crowds with my eyes turned down? Why didn't I give my money all to charity?

SCROOGE: Don't be flowery, Jacob.

MARLEY'S GHOST: Hear me. My time is nearly gone. I am here to warn you.

SCROOGE: You were always a good friend to me, Jacob.

MARLEY'S GHOST: You may yet have a chance to escape my fate.

SCROOGE: Thank'ee.

MARLEY'S GHOST: You will be haunted... by three spirits.

SCROOGE: Is that the hope you mentioned, Jacob?

MARLEY'S GHOST: It is.

SCROOGE: Then I think I'd better not.

MARLEY'S GHOST: You have no choice. Expect the first one when the bell tolls one.

SCROOGE: Couldn't I take 'em at once and have it over, Jacob?

MARLEY'S GHOST: Expect the second when the bell tolls two.

SCROOGE: But Jacob...

MARLEY'S GHOST: Expect the third...

(There is ghostly laughter off.)

SCROOGE: What's that?

MARLEY'S GHOST: For your own sake, Scrooge, remember what has passed between us. Look.

(Marley's Ghost disappears, and lights pick up the Ghost of Christmas Past... a strange figure like a child... yet more like an old man... white hair hung around its neck... dressed in white... a branch of holly in its hand... a bright clear jet of light issuing from its head.)

SCROOGE: Jacob... Jacob... help me... Jacob. *(Searches frantically but Jacob has gone)*

FIRST GHOST: I think you'd better talk to me.

SCROOGE: Who are you?

FIRST GHOST: I am the Ghost of Christmas Past.

SCROOGE: Long past?

FIRST GHOST: Your past. Rise and walk with me.

SCROOGE: No, no, I can't.

FIRST GHOST: It's your only hope of being saved.

SCROOGE: Let me go.

FIRST GHOST: Come... we have far to go.

SCROOGE: It's bitter cold outside.

FIRST GHOST: What matter?

SCROOGE: I have no coat.

FIRST GHOST: No one can wither your cold spirit... come. *(Weird laughter... Scrooge clasps the Ghost's robe.)*

SCROOGE: I am a mortal... I'll fall.

FIRST GHOST: Come with me.

SCROOGE: No... no.

(There is a murmur of ghostly voices... the lights whirl... a loud sweeping noise of wind... and Scrooge's wail.)

CURTAIN

ACT TWO
SCENE ONE

(The same wind that was heard at the close of Act One sweeps up again. The First Ghost and Scrooge are spotted high up. They stand on step ladders behind a velvet curtain. Below is a "long, bare, melancholy room made barer by lines of plain deal forms and desks.")

SCROOGE: Help. Help. I'm falling!

FIRST GHOST: Stand up.

SCROOGE: I'm falling, hold me!

FIRST GHOST: You haven't lost your feet, man. Stand up.

SCROOGE: There. That's better. Where are we now?

FIRST GHOST: You've been here many times before.

SCROOGE: I see nothing but darkness.

FIRST GHOST: Your eyes will grow accustomed to looking back in time.

(A burst of boyish laughter is heard. Several boys are spotted... suitcases and caps in hand.)

GEORGE: *(Throwing cap in air)* No more school for two whole weeks. Hooray!

ROB: Where are you going to spend Christmas, Freddie?

FRED: We always go to my grandmother's. Where you going?

ROB: My father's taking me up to London.

FRED: That's great. Come along, the carriage will be waiting.

GEORGE: Rob and I are waiting till my mother comes. Good-bye.

ALL THREE: Good-bye... Merry Christmas.

ROB: I say, George... wouldn't it be awful to stay at this old school at Christmas time?

GEORGE: What if you didn't have a home... or a mother?

ROB: It's terrible even to think about...

GEORGE: Oh, I forgot a book... wait here while I get it.

(Spot up on First Ghost and Scrooge.)

FIRST GHOST: Now do you know where you are, Scrooge?

SCROOGE: Yes. Yes, I know. It's my old school. Everybody's going home for the holidays.

FIRST GHOST: Everybody?

SCROOGE: No... there is one boy left alone...

(Spot drops to stage... a boy is sitting at a desk, head in arms, sobbing. George looks in.)

GEORGE: Oh, I beg your pardon... I thought everyone had gone. I just came in for a book. I say, it's young Scrooge. You aren't crying, are you?

YOUNG SCROOGE: No.

GEORGE: Why didn't you take the carriage with the others?

YOUNG SCROOGE: Why should I?

GEORGE: Aren't you going home?

YOUNG SCROOGE: No.

GEORGE: Everybody goes home at Christmas time.

YOUNG SCROOGE: I'm not.

GEORGE: Don't you have a home?

YOUNG SCROOGE: No.

GEORGE: You have a father.

YOUNG SCROOGE: No.

GEORGE: You have, too. I saw him bring you up to school this
  fall.

YOUNG SCROOGE: What good's a father if he doesn't let you come
  home?

GEORGE: Oh, I say, that's beastly. What are you going to do?

YOUNG SCROOGE: Stay here.

GEORGE: But you'll be all alone.

YOUNG SCROOGE: The housekeeper is going to stay. She'll give
  me meals.

GEORGE: Yes, I suppose she will. Well, I've got to hurry along.
  My mother's calling for me in the carriage. Merry Christmas.

YOUNG SCROOGE: Merry... *(He can't finish... but sobs, and
  George runs out. Spot up on First Ghost and Scrooge)*

SCROOGE: Please take me away, Ghost... take me away.

FIRST GHOST: Aren't you feeling well?

SCROOGE: I don't want to remember... I can't bear to remember...
  take me away.

FIRST GHOST: Stay. It is my duty to show you the things of the
  past.

*(There is a knocking below... the schoolroom is spotted again. A
little girl, Fan, enters.)*

FAN: I beg your pardon... I'm looking for my brother.

YOUNG SCROOGE: There's no one here.

FAN: His name is Scrooge. Ebenezer Scrooge... Could you tell
  me...

YOUNG SCROOGE: Fan!

FAN: *(She rushes to him.)* My brother. I thought I'd never find
  you. I've looked everywhere. I've come to take you home.

YOUNG SCROOGE: Home?

FAN: Yes, home. Don't stare so... I've come to take you home.

YOUNG SCROOGE: Is Father dead?

FAN: He sent me for you. He's much kinder than he used to be. He spoke to me so kindly one night when I was starting to bed that I wasn't afraid to ask him once more if you might come home.

YOUNG SCROOGE: And he said yes?

FAN: He even sent me in a carriage to bring you. And we're to be together all the Christmas long. Hurry... come on... oh, I'm so excited I can hardly talk.

(She drags him off and the lights change back to the First Ghost and Scrooge.)

SCROOGE: That was the only happy Christmas I ever had. My sister died.

FIRST GHOST: She left a child, didn't she?

SCROOGE: Yes, one.

FIRST GHOST: Your nephew. What have you done for him? Have you loved him dearly for your sister's sake?

SCROOGE: Take me away, I don't want to remember any more.

FIRST GHOST: You have no choice. My orders are to show you the Christmas Past.

(There is a moaning of wind... a flashing of lights... a spot steadies itself on the opposite side of the room where the Ghost and Scrooge can see without moving.)

ACT TWO
SCENE TWO

(Fezziwig sits at his desk. Looking at watch, he leans back and laughs from his shoes to his organ of benevolence.)

SCROOGE: Why, it's old Fezziwig. Bless his heart. It's Fezziwig alive again.

FIRST GHOST: Then you recall this place.

SCROOGE: Recall it? I was apprenticed here. I learned here all I know of business.

FIRST GHOST: All? Did Mr. Fezziwig treat you the way you treat your clerk?

FEZZIWIG: Yo... ho, there. Ebenezer... Dick!

(Young Ebenezer Scrooge and Dick run in.)

FEZZIWIG: Yo, ho, my boys. No more work tonight. Christmas Eve, Dick. Christmas, Ebenezer. Let's have the shutters up before a man can say Jack Robinson.

(The two young men rush out and Fezziwig skips down from his desk.)

FEZZIWIG: Hilli... ho. Christmas. Only comes once a year. Worth waiting for. Worth celebrating. Worth remembering.

EBENEZER: *(Rushing back with Dick, both panting)* The shutters are up, sir. Now what?

FEZZIWIG: Clear everything away, lads. Let's have lots of room here. Hilli ho, Dick. Chirrip, Ebenezer.

EBENEZER: I'll sweep the floor, Dick. You trim the lamps.

FEZZIWIG: And call in the fiddler. There's going to be a party. A dance. Festivities. Hilli ho... the fiddler.

FIDDLER: *(Hurrying in, bowing)* Heard you the minute you spoke, sir.

FEZZIWIG: Merry Christmas. Merry Christmas. Make yourself right at home. Take any seat you like.

FIDDLER: I'll just take over this desk if you don't mind, sir.

FEZZIWIG: Anything you like... anything. Make yourself comfortable.

FIDDLER: *(Putting up music stand and spreading music)* Hope everyone's feeling frisky. Fine night for dancing. *(He tunes up like fifty stomach aches.)*

EBENEZER: Here's Mrs. Fezziwig, sir.

FEZZIWIG: Ah, madame.

(He bows low as Mrs. F comes in, one vast substantial smile.)

MRS. F: Good evening, dear. Good evening, boys, Ebenezer, Dick.

BOYS: Good evening, Mrs. Fezziwig.

FEZZIWIG: You're looking very beautiful tonight, madame.

MRS. F: Now, Fezziwig. When you begin such flattery, I always know you're wanting something.

FEZZIWIG: *(Roars with laughter)* Finest wife a man ever had, boys. *(To her)* Is everything ready for supper?

MRS. F: Gracious. I hope so, and I hope there's enough.

FEZZIWIG: Any oysters?

MRS. F: Oysters... and plum pudding.

FEZZIWIG: Mince pie?

MRS. F: Don't I always have mince pie? And pumpkin pie? How many do you think will be here?

FEZZIWIG: Twenty... forty... as many as like. Any cakes?

MRS. F: Let me see. Chocolate cake... marshmallow cake... banana cake and spice cake. Is that enough?

FEZZIWIG: Yes, but don't we get anything except dessert?

MRS. F: You'd think you'd never had enough to eat the way your ribs stick out. *(Mr. Fezziwig roars with laughter again.)* There's cold roast and turkey and sausages and chestnuts.

FEZZIWIG: Yo ho... and hilli... ho... it makes my mouth water... how about you, boys? Well, let's get on with the dancing... you ready there, fiddler?

FIDDLER: Ready, sir.

FEZZIWIG: You aren't going to be all tired out after the first dance, are you?

FIDDLER: I can play as long as you can shake a leg, sir.

FEZZIWIG: *(Laughing)* Everybody... step this way... music's about to begin. *(All line up.)* All right, Fiddler, let her go!

(As Fezziwig calls "All right, Fiddler" the dancers begin. Young Scrooge, however, holds back, anxiously watching the door and consulting his watch. The dance ends.)

FEZZIWIG: I call halt... well done... well done! You, Scrooge, give the fiddler something to drink.

EBENEZER: Here you are, sir.

(Fiddler grabs the pot of porter as Scrooge sees Charlotte coming through the door. He rushes to her, takes her hand.)

EBENEZER: You're late. I thought you'd never come.

(Charlotte is gay and pretty. Obviously in love with Scrooge. She takes his hand and pulls him with her to Fezziwig.)

CHARLOTTE: Merry Christmas, Mr. Fezziwig.

FEZZIWIG: Well bless my stars, if it isn't Charlotte.

CHARLOTTE: I'm sorry to be so late, sir.

FEZZIWIG: Quite all right, quite all right... except that it's made young Scrooge here mighty nervous. *(Scrooge and Charlotte laugh.)* But I guess he'll recover after he's danced with you. You there, Fiddler. Need any more rest?

FIDDLER: Me? Rest?

(He strikes up a fast tune, "Roger de Coverly." The dancers gather.)

EBENEZER: I say, Mr. Fezziwig should lead this dance.

(Crowd shouts.)

FEZZIWIG: I consider this an honor. *(Bows to Mrs. F)* Madame. Ready, Fiddler.

(All dance.)

FEZZIWIG: *(At close of dance, he roars)* Step this way... there's everything to tempt the appetite. There's cold roast and cold boiled. There's mince pies and pumpkin pies. Merry Christmas, everyone... come along.

(All troupe off... but Scrooge pulls Charlotte back. Blackout. Spot picks up First Ghost and Scrooge.)

SCROOGE: We must follow them, Ghost.

FIRST GHOST: Why?

SCROOGE: I want to see them, they're all so happy.

FIRST GHOST: You seem to be enjoying yourself.

SCROOGE: I am... I am... and so are all the others.

FIRST GHOST: Ho... hum... I can't see what Mr. Fezziwig has done to make them all so happy.

SCROOGE: He's done everything.

FIRST GHOST: What's he done? Used his own warehouse for a dance. Hasn't spent more than a few pounds on the whole party.

SCROOGE: What difference does that make? The happiness he gives is quite as great as if he spent a fortune.

FIRST GHOST: How did you ever forget these things in your later years?

(Bell tolls. The spot picks up Scrooge and Charlotte. Scrooge seems older, "a man in the prime of life." His face has not the harsh and rigid lines of later years but it has begun to wear the signs of care and avarice. There's an eager, greedy, restless motion in his eye.)

EBENEZER: *(To Charlotte)* Why do you tell me you won't marry me... after so many years?

CHARLOTTE: You do not love me any more

EBENEZER: You are my idol.

CHARLOTTE: I think I was... once... long ago when we were young and you were a poor clerk for Mr. Fezziwig. Your idol now is gold.

EBENEZER: *(Preening himself)* Is it a sin to escape poverty?

CHARLOTTE: No... it isn't a sin to escape poverty.

EBENEZER: Come then. What's troubling you? I haven't asked to be released from marrying you, have I?

CHARLOTTE: No, not in words. But I've seen your love of gold grow like a mighty passion till nothing else matters to you. Tell me, if you were free now, would you ask to marry a poor girl like me?

(Scrooge turns away searching for an answer. He knows he wouldn't, yet he doesn't care to admit it.)

CHARLOTTE: It's as I thought. *(She starts to leave.)*

EBENEZER: Charlotte!

CHARLOTTE: May you be happy in the life you have chosen. *(She slips away.)*

EBENEZER: *(He starts half-heartedly after her.)* Charlotte...

(A bell starts tolling. The spot picks up old Scrooge and the Ghost.)

SCROOGE: *(Desperately)* Why do you delight to torture me? I never should have let her go.

FIRST GHOST: Listen.

(The bell tolls.)

SCROOGE: Show me no more!

FIRST GHOST: I must. *(Wails in a fearful manner)*

SCROOGE: What's the matter?

FIRST GHOST: My time is up. Farewell.

SCROOGE: Don't leave me here... don't leave me.

(The bell strikes two. There is hollow laughter.)

FIRST GHOST: He's come. I cannot stay.

SCROOGE: Don't leave me. Take me with you.

FIRST GHOST: Stay.

(He sweeps off in a moan of wind. The next Ghost appears... "dressed in a simple, dark green robe bordered with white fur. He wears a wreath of holly on his head. An antique scabbard without a sword hangs at his side." Scrooge does not look.)

SECOND GHOST: Look upon me.

SCROOGE: No... no.

SECOND GHOST: Look.

SCROOGE: Oh, please go 'way.

SECOND GHOST: You've never seen the like of me before.

SCROOGE: I've seen enough tonight... please go.

SECOND GHOST: Touch my robe.

SCROOGE: Please do not ask me.

SECOND GHOST: Touch my robe. I am the Ghost of Christmas Present. Come with me.

(A carol begins in background.)

SCROOGE: I cannot go with you... I have seen too much already.

SECOND GHOST: You are to see all the world you live in.

(Blackout... The carol continues.)

ACT TWO
SCENE THREE

(Lights up on the Cratchit kitchen. Mrs. C. and Belinda are putting the finishing touches to the feast.)

MRS. C: *(Standing back to survey the dinner table)* There we are. Everything is almost ready. I wish we were having a turkey, but we'll make the best of what we have.

BELINDA: You always have fine dinners, Mother.

MRS. C: Thank you, dear. What do you suppose has happened to Martha?

BELINDA: She's coming now... *(Rushes to door... there is no one.)*

MRS. C: Dear me!

BELINDA: I must be hearing things. When you want someone to come very much every minute seems like an hour.

MRS. C: She'll be coming presently. Oh, I should have asked Peter to blow the fire a bit.

BELINDA: I'll ask him. *(Calls out the door)* Peter. Peter, Mother wants you to blow up the fire.

PETER: Coming. *(He enters elegantly attired in his father's shirt... the corners of his monstrous collar always getting in his mouth.)*

BELINDA and MRS C: *(Gasping)* Peter!

PETER: *(Turning around proudly)* Well?

BELINDA: Where did you get those clothes, Peter Cratchit?

PETER: Father loaned them to me in honor of Christmas.

MRS. C: Well, I must say you look like a grown man.

PETER: I'm almost a man. Father thinks he can get me a situation where I'll earn five and sixpence every week.

MRS. C: Splendid, dear. Turn around again and let me look at you.

PETER: *(Turning)* I thought I might take a walk in the park later.

BELINDA: You mustn't let him go, Mother.

PETER: And why not?

BELINDA: First thing you know some lady will see him and then he'll be keeping company and setting up housekeeping for himself.

PETER: Get along with you. Was it the fire wanted fixing, Mother?

MRS. C: Here. You can't be blowing fires with all those good clothes on. I'll fix it.

PETER: *(Holding her back)* No you won't. Just watch me.

BELINDA: Listen. That must be Martha coming now.

(She runs to the door. Edward and Elizabeth rush in, nearly knocking her over.)

EDWARD and ELIZABETH: We smelled it... we smelled it... we knew it was ours.

MRS. C: Bless us. Smelled what?

BOTH: The goose.

PETER: What goose.

BOTH: Our goose.

PETER: We haven't a goose... have we, Belinda?

BELINDA: I'm sure I haven't seen a goose walking around.

BOTH: Well, it wouldn't be walking around.

PETER: What else could a goose do?
EDWARD: Mother, make him stop.

PETER: I'm not doing a thing, Mother.

ELIZABETH: We do have a goose, don't we, Mother?

EDWARD: Don't we? Tell us... don't we?

PETER: How can anybody tell us don't we?

BOTH: Oh—you! *(They rush him and jump on him.)*

PETER: Hey, Mother. Get away, you. Mother, make them get away.

MRS. C: Children... children. Edward... Elizabeth. *(She and Belinda pull them off. Peter rearranges his clothes haughtily.)* Peter's all dressed up for dinner.

EDWARD: Then why'd he say we don't have a goose?

PETER: Can't you take a joke?

EDWARD: Does it have sage and onions stuffed in it?

MRS. C: Wait and see. Wait and see.

(Edward and Elizabeth dance around the table chanting.)

EDWARD and ELIZABETH: We have a goose. We have a goose. We have a goose for dinner!

MRS. C: Run along and wash your hands... both of you.

EDWARD: How long before we eat?

MRS. C: Not long.

ELIZABETH: I want to eat right now. I'm so hungry I can't wait.

BELINDA: We have to wait for Martha, sillies.

BOTH: Will Martha bring us a present?

BELINDA: Don't you ever think of anything but presents?

PETER: And don't start asking her the minute she walks in the door.

BELINDA: There she is coming this time, I'm sure. *(Opens door)* She's here, Mother, she's here.

MRS. C: *(Feeling her hair and brushing her apron)* Dear me. I should have looked in a mirror.

BELINDA: Martha, darling. We've waited hours.

MARTHA: Merry Christmas, everyone. *(She drops packages. The little ones pick them up.)*

EDWARD: There's a goose, Martha. Smell it.

MARTHA: I've been smelling it all the way down the block. *(Hugs her mother.)* Dearest Mother.

MRS. C: Bless your heart alive. You look tired.

MARTHA: We had such a lot of work to do.

EDWARD: Anything in here for us?

PETER: Edward!

EDWARD: Well, it doesn't hurt to ask, does it?

MARTHA: Here, this one is for you... and this for you, Elizabeth.

PETER: I don't know why nobody ever speaks to me.

MARTHA: Peter, darling. *(Rushes to hug him... then leans back to look at him.)* But I shouldn't be expected to know you... all dressed up... I thought some handsome stranger had come to join the party.

PETER: *(Pulls at his collar self-consciously)* Thank you, Martha.

MARTHA: *(Addressing all but Peter)* I saw a countess and a lord some days ago... and his lordship was just about as tall as Peter. Only not half so handsome.

EDWARD and ELIZABETH: Peter's handsome as his lordship... Peter's handsome.

PETER: *(Grabs them)* Here, you.

EDWARD: Be careful. You'll break our gingerbread men.

ELIZABETH: Look, Mother... Martha brought us gingerbread men.

EDWARD: Want a bite anybody? Want a bite? *(Offers one to each)*

MRS. C: Stop the noise, children... Here, dear. *(To Martha)* Give me your shawl and bonnet. It's good to have you, dear.

MARTHA: I would have come last night, but being apprenticed to a milliner isn't easy. We had to work all last evening and clear away this morning.

MRS. C: Never mind so long as you're here now. Sit down by the fire. Your hands are like ice.

MARTHA: Where's Father? And Tiny Tim?

MRS. C: I'd like to know myself. They've been out the whole blessed morning.

MARTHA: Mother, how is Tim?

MRS. C: No better, Martha... no better.

(Tears spring to her eyes and she turns to brush them away with her apron. Martha puts her arms around her. The others follow.)

MARTHA: There, dear. I didn't mean to make you sad.

MRS. C: It's all right. Just got a little smoke in my eyes... that stove smokes badly.

PETER: Oh, very badly.

EDWARD: Tim was throwing snowballs this morning.

ELIZABETH: We made them for him.

MRS. C: It was nice of you, darling, and I don't mean to worry, only he shouldn't be out so long in the cold.

PETER: Father took him to church.

BELINDA: He won't be cold in there.

MRS. C: Of course he won't, and Father would take good care of him anyway. Now let's see that everything is ready for dinner.

EDWARD: Here comes Father now.

ELIZABETH: Hide, Martha.

EDWARD: Yes, hide. Father will think you aren't here.

ELIZABETH: You can surprise him.

MARTHA: *(To her mother)* Do you think I should?

(Mrs. C. nods "yes.")

EDWARD: Hurry. Hide.

ELIZABETH: They're coming.

MARTHA: Where can I hide?

BELINDA: Behind the door.

EDWARD: No, that won't do.

ELIZABETH: They'll see you there.

MARTHA: Where? Where?

EDWARD: Under a chair.

MARTHA: I'll spoil my dress.

EDWARD: Hide some place. Hurry.

PETER: Get in the cupboard.

EDWARD and ELIZABETH: Yes. Get in the cupboard.

MARTHA: Help me.

(They squeeze Martha into a cupboard. Elizabeth holds the front door closed and dances up and down frantically.)

EDWARD: Don't you say a word, Mother.

PETER: All ready? Open the door.

BELINDA: Everybody pretend to be doing something.

(They each get busy. Bob comes in carrying Tiny Tim.)

BOB: Clear the way for the fastest horse in the country.

TIM: Whoa there. Whoa. Steady, boy, steady.

(Bob slows up with difficulty. Tim laughs merrily. Peter lifts him down.)

MRS. C: I declare, I thought you two were going to be late for dinner.

BOB: We wouldn't be late for one of Mrs. Cratchit's dinners, would we, Tim?

TIM: No, we wouldn't be late.

(Edward and Elizabeth have been popping with excitement... holding their hands over their mouths to keep from bursting with laughter. Bob sees them.)

BOB: What's the matter with you two?

MRS. C: They've smelled the goose and can hardly contain themselves.

BOB: Hasn't our Martha come yet?

BELINDA: She's not coming.

BOB: Not coming!

TIM: Not coming!

PETER: It's a rotten shame, I say.

BOB: Wouldn't they let her take the day off?

(Martha looks out of the cabinet.)

PETER: That milliner she works for is meaner than Scrooge.

BOB: But it's terrible. Everybody should have Christmas Day. *(Puts his head in his hands)*

MRS. C: There, dear.

BOB: I've been looking forward so to seeing Martha.

MRS. C: We'll just have to make the best of it.

BELINDA: Seems to me the rest of us ought to go right ahead being happy.

(Bob sits quietly. Martha is tiptoeing up behind him. She puts her hands over his eyes.)

EDWARD: Guess who... guess who it is...

BOB: Starting Blindman's Buff early, are you? Now let me see, it's Belinda.

BELINDA: Guess again... guess again.

BOB: It isn't Tim?

EDWARD: No, it isn't Tim.

BELINDA: Guess again... guess again.

BOB: Is it you, Mother?

MRS. C: Gracious. You could feel the scars and burns on my hands.

BOB: Is it Peter?

PETER: Do you think I'd have such soft white hands?

BOB: I can't see the color of your hands. Is it you, Edward?

EDWARD: Here I am. Can't you hear me?

BOB: Then that leaves Elizabeth.

ELIZABETH: *(Choking with delight)* It isn't me... it isn't me. Guess again.

BOB: It can't be... it can't be... Martha!

MARTHA: *(Hugging him)* Why can't it be Martha?

EDWARD: We fooled you... we fooled you.

ELIZABETH: Father thought she wasn't coming.

MARTHA: Darling Father. It was mean of us to tease you.

BOB: I ought to know better than to listen to those two young scalawags.

EDWARD: We're scalawags... we're scalawags.

(They turn somersaults in glee.)

BOB: Well, now it is a perfect Christmas.

MARTHA: *(To Tim)* And how's my little brother?

TIM: I threw a snowball as far as Peter... almost.

PETER: That's what he did.

TIM: Someday I'll throw one farther!

MARTHA: Of course you will, darling.

EDWARD: Tim, do you want to smell something good?

TIM: What is it?

EDWARD: Come with us, we'll let you smell it.

ELIZABETH: It'll smell so good you won't be able to wait to eat it.

MRS. C: I smell something burning.

PETER: The potatoes... help! *(Runs to stove and grabs pan)*

MRS. C: Wash your hands and hurry back, children.

(The two exit with Tim.)

PETER: Want me to mash these potatoes?

MRS. C: Well, they mustn't have any lumps in them.

PETER: The very idea. Why, I'm the best potato masher in town.

MARTHA: What can I do?

MRS. C: You sit right there and talk to your father.

MARTHA: Did you really take Tim to church, Father?

BOB: He asked to go, and he was good as gold. Only he gets to thinking such strange things.

MARTHA: What kind of things?

BOB: Coming home, he told me he hoped all the people in church saw him, because he was a cripple. He thought it might help them to remember who made lame beggars walk and blind men see.

MARTHA: God bless his heart. He looks quite pale.

BOB: I hope I didn't keep him out too long.

MARTHA: Of course you didn't.

MRS. C: Don't forget it's your job to stir the punch, Mr. Cratchit.

BOB: My goodness, yes. We can't make toasts without hot punch.

MRS. C: Martha, you put on the plates. Belinda, you sweeten the applesauce.

(The children return.)

EDWARD: Where's the goose?

MRS. C: You put the chairs around the table and Peter will get the goose.

(Edward and Elizabeth put chairs up... sit down and put spoons in their mouths.)

BOB: Here, Tim, you sit right here beside me.

MRS. C: What are you children doing with spoons in your mouths?

EDWARD: Keeping them in so we can't ask for goose before it's our turn.

ELIZABETH: Here it comes... here it comes.

(Peter carries the goose in.)

MRS. C: Sit down, everybody. Sit down.

BELINDA: I'm pouring punch into the cups.

BOB: Good. Then we shall each one make a toast.

EDWARD: I make a toast to our goose.

ALL: The goose.

BOB: And I make a toast to the lady who cooked the goose.

PETER: To the finest mother in the world.

ALL: To Mother... to Mrs. Cratchit.

MRS. C: *(Holding up her cup)* A Merry Christmas to us all, my
  dears.

ALL: A Merry Christmas to us all.

TIM: God bless us every one.

BOB: And I will give you Mr. Scrooge, the founder of the feast.

MRS. C: *(Sitting down)* Founder of the feast, indeed. I wish I had
  him here, I'd give him a piece of my mind to feast upon and I
  hope he'd have a good appetite for it.

BOB: My dear, it's Christmas Day.

MRS. C: It should be Christmas Day, I'm sure, when one drinks
  the health of such an odious, stingy, hard, unfeeling man as Mr.
  Scrooge.

BOB: He may not be so hard.
MRS. C: You know better than anyone else how hard he is.

PETER: It makes me feel awful just to hear his name.

OTHERS: Me, too.

MRS. C: Forgive me, dear... that man is such an ogre in my life that I steam up like a pudding the minute I hear his name.

BOB: It's Christmas Day.

MRS. C: *(Gets up)* I'll drink his health for your sake and the day's long life to him. A Merry Christmas and a Happy New Year. He'll be very merry and very happy, I have no doubt.

OTHERS: A Merry Christmas.

BOB: *(Lifting knife)* And now the goose.

(Cheers from everyone... blackout on the family... spot on Scrooge and the Second Ghost.)

SCROOGE: Did you hear them, Ghost? Did you hear? They drank a toast to me...

SECOND GHOST: It wasn't such a hearty one.

SCROOGE: Ghost, tell me... tell me if Tiny Tim will live...

SECOND GHOST: I see a vacant chair in that poor room... a crutch without an owner... carefully preserved. If these shadows remain unaltered by the future, Tiny Tim will die.

SCROOGE: No... no. He mustn't die.

CURTAIN

ACT THREE
SCENE ONE

(A graveyard... a tombstone... gleaming in a weird light. A bell tolls three. Scrooge stumbles on alone, and very frightened. There are eerie sounds. From nowhere a phantom, shrouded in black, appears. Only his hand is visible. He neither moves nor speaks. Scrooge falls to his knees.)

SCROOGE: I came here as you told me to. But it's a fearful place. Are you the Ghost of Christmas yet to come?

(The Ghost waves a hand.)

SCROOGE: You are about to show me things which will happen in the future? Is that so, spirit? Have you no tongue to speak?

(The Third Ghost shakes his hand.)

SCROOGE: Ghost of the future, I fear you more than any spectre I have seen. But I know you intend to do me good, so I'll go with you and do it with a thankful heart. Now will you speak to me?

(Third Ghost points to the stone.)

SCROOGE: Whose grave is this? Why did you bring me here? *(He stoops to read.)* Ebenezer Scrooge. No, no, it cannot be. I'm Scrooge. I'm not dead. I'm not. And yet, someday I will be dead. Ghost, what is it you want to show me?

(The Third Ghost motions for him to move back. A spry old rascal rushes in and sits cross legged on the grave, leaning against the stone. A woman enters, dragging a heavy bundle.)

JOE: I see you weren't afraid to come.

CHARWOMAN: A fine place to ask a decent self-respecting woman to meet you. A graveyard.

JOE: It's a healthy enough place for the likes of you, and no one about to tell tales.

CHARWOMAN: Well, look at what I brought.

JOE: We'll wait for the others.

CHARWOMAN: You didn't tell me anyone else was coming. Who is it?

JOE: You can see for yourself in a minute. The lady's a friend of yours.

(The laundress stumbles in.)
JOE: You're late.

LAUNDRESS: Praise the saints I got here at all. How's a body to see in this pitch darkness? *(Sees charwoman)* Who's that?

JOE: By name, Mrs. Dilber... one cleaning woman for a Mr. Scrooge.
LAUNDRESS: What are you doing here?

CHARWOMAN: Same thing as you. I see you've got a bundle too.

LAUNDRESS: Well, it's no sin, taking a few things from a dead man what can't have no use for them any more.

MAN: *(Calling off)* Joe. Hey, Joe. You there?

JOE: This way. Over here.

CHARWOMAN: Who's coming now?

JOE: Only the undertaker's man.

MAN: It's the devil's own place you pick for meeting.

JOE: Only place our friend could be buried in.

LAUNDRESS: *(Leaping back)* You don't mean this is the place he's buried?

JOE: Why not? Seems only fitting and proper I should be sitting on his grave while I look over his own belongings.

CHARWOMAN: Get to the looking then. I don't like this place.

LAUNDRESS: Me neither.

CHARWOMAN: I'd swear spooks was watching us.

(There is a burst of weird laughter.)

MAN: What was that?

JOE: That was me, laughing. Old Ebenezer Scrooge. Frightened everyone away from him when he was alive. Didn't have a single soul at his funeral.

LAUNDRESS: He didn't never have a kind word for no one. Me, I don't know why I kept on doing his washing.

CHARWOMAN: Wouldn't let his nephew come near him even.

LAUNDRESS: And that poor clerk of his... oh, my.

CHARWOMAN: And as for Christmas... he never had a respectful word for Christmas.

JOE: Died without a friend and we're the ones to profit by it. Ho... ho. Well, show me what you've brought and I'll pay fairly for it.

MAN: I'm first.

CHARWOMAN: I got here first.

JOE: Charwoman's first. Open your bundle. Well, don't act as if you were scared out of your wits. Nobody's going to pick your pockets around here.

CHARWOMAN: I hope. Well, there you are.

JOE: Blankets. Well, upon my word. That's rich. You didn't take the blankets off the poor man's bed, did you?

CHARWOMAN: Why not? He didn't need 'em any more.

LAUNDRESS: That's what I say. I've got his best shirt.

MAN: And I've got his boots and cuff links.

JOE: What a miserable end for Ebenezer Scrooge.

(Ghostly laughter. Lights up on Ghost and Scrooge. Others slip off.)

SCROOGE: Merciful Heaven. Take me away from here, Ghost. Please take me away. In leaving this place I'll not forget the lessons it has taught. *(He leans on the stone.)* Poor man, not a soul to mourn for him... and it was all his own fault. Ghost, if you can see the future, show me what's happened to Tiny Tim.

(The Third Ghost waves his hand. They move across with the spot. The stone is taken away and the lights come up on the Cratchit kitchen.)

ACT THREE
SCENE TWO

(The Third Ghost and Scrooge move to one side out of the light. Mrs. Cratchit sits with the children around her... all except Tiny Tim. They are all quiet and sad. Peter has been reading to them.)

PETER: *(Reading)* ... and he took a child and set him in the midst of them.

(Mrs. C. drops her sewing and hides her face in her hands. Martha puts her arm around her.)

MARTHA: There, dear, don't cry. Our Tim is happy now... he'll never have to be sick any more.

MRS. C: It's just the sewing hurts my eyes. *(Wipes them hastily)* They're better now. It makes them weak by candle light. *(Gets up)* But I wouldn't show weak eyes to your father when he comes home for the world.

MARTHA: It's near his time.

PETER: Past it. But I think he's walked a little slower than he used to these last few evenings.

MRS. C: I have known him to walk with... I have known him to walk with Tiny Tim on his shoulder very fast, indeed.

BELINDA: And so have I... often.

EDWARD: And so have I.

MRS. C: But Tim was very light to carry... and his father loved him so that it was no trouble... no trouble.

BELINDA: I think he's coming now.

MRS. C: Put the kettle on for his tea... he'll need warming. And we must each one do our best to make him feel cheerful.

MARTHA: Our Tim would have it so.

(She opens the door and hugs Bob as he enters. The others rush up to greet him.)
MARTHA: We're glad you've come, Father.

EDWARD: I'll take your hat.

ELIZABETH: I'll hang your scarf up.

BELINDA: I'm making your tea, Father.

MRS. C: *(Embracing him)* Good evening, dear.

PETER: Have a good day, Father?

MRS. C: Come dear, sit by the fire.

(He sits down... the youngest sit on the floor and lean on his knees. Martha and Peter lean on his shoulders. Belinda pours a cup of tea.)

BOB: I met Mr. Scrooge's nephew on the street today. He stopped to ask me why I looked so down. "Surely," he said, "not because my Uncle Scrooge is gone."

PETER: Nobody could feel badly about his being gone.

MRS. C: What else did Scrooge's nephew say?

BOB: He asked me why I looked sad, then... and he said it so kindly that I told him... I told him about Tim. And he stepped right up and put his hand on my shoulder and said, "I'm heartily sorry for it, Mr. Cratchit... and heartily sorry for your good wife too." By the by, how he ever knew that I don't know.

MRS. C: Knew what, dear?

BOB: That you were a good wife.

PETER: Everybody knows that.

BOB: Well observed, my boy. I hope they do. Well, Mr. Scrooge's nephew said, "I'm heartily sorry for your good wife. If I can be

of service to you in any way, here's my card. That's where I live."
(Shows card to Mrs. C.)

MRS. C: What a fine gentleman he must be.

MARTHA: Not like his uncle Scrooge at all.

BOB: You couldn't tell he was a nephew. The kind way he spoke you'd think he knew our Tim.

MRS. C: I'm sure he's a good soul.

BOB: You know, I wouldn't be a bit surprised if he gets Peter a better situation.

BELINDA: Oh dear, if Peter gets a better situation he'll surely be getting married.

PETER: You don't need to worry... I'm not going to leave here.

MRS. C: Likely as not you will be one of these days... though there's plenty of time for that.

BOB: But however and whenever we part from one another... I am sure we shall none of us forget poor Tiny Tim... or this first parting that there was among us.

(Mrs. C. cries softly.)

ALL: Never, Father.

BOB: Tim was such a little child. We shall never quarrel among ourselves and forget our Tim in doing it.

ALL: Not ever, Father.

BOB: Then I am very happy... *(Mrs. C. kisses him.)* Yes, very happy.

(Spot picks up Scrooge and the Ghost... the others slip away.)

SCROOGE: Poor Tiny Tim. I could have helped him. Ghost, are these the shadows of things that will be... or is it possible to change the future?

(The Third Ghost merely waves a hand.)

SCROOGE: Why show me this if I am past all hope? Surely there is something I can do. I will honor Christmas in my heart and try to keep it all the year. I will live in the past, the present and the future. I will not shut out the lessons they teach... oh, speak to me. Give me some hope. Tell me that I may still have time to change.

(He catches at the Third Ghost who moves steadily away. Scrooge falls to the floor. Blackout.)

ACT THREE
SCENE THREE

(The unit set for the office is moved on. Bells are clanging and snatches of carols are heard. Lights come up on Scrooge sitting at his desk, head down in arms.)

SCROOGE: Don't leave me, Ghost... give me some hope... tell me it is not too late. *(He sits up.)* This is my office... how did I get here? Everything looks just the same as always. Am I dreaming? I feel light as a feather. Do you suppose that I'm an angel? What day is this? What day? I don't know what day of the month it is... I must find out what day it is. *(Bells ring outside... Scrooge rushes to the door and calls out.)* Hello out there! Hello... come in here a minute. Come in. *(Peter Cratchit enters hesitantly.)* Don't be afraid. Come in.

PETER: Yes, sir.

SCROOGE: What's today?

PETER: Sir?

SCROOGE: What day's today, my fine fellow?

PETER: Today? Why, it's Christmas Day.

SCROOGE: Christmas Day? Are you sure?

PETER: Yes, sir.

SCROOGE: Positive?

PETER: Positive.

SCROOGE: Then I haven't missed it. The spirits have done it all in one night. Wonderful things, spirits. They can do anything they like. Of course they can... *(He leaps in the air.)* Of course they can. *(Suddenly he grabs Peter's hand and shakes it violently.)* Hello, my fine fellow... no, no, don't go away... what's your name?

PETER: Peter Cra...

SCROOGE: Peter... charming name... wonderful name. Peter, do you know the grocer's down the street?

PETER: Yes, sir.

SCROOGE: An intelligent boy... a remarkable boy. Do you know whether they've sold the prize turkey that was hanging up there? Not the little prize turkey, the big one?

PETER: You mean the one almost as big as me?

SCROOGE: What a delightful boy. It's a pleasure to talk to you. Yes, my buck, the one almost as big as you.

PETER: It's still hanging there.

SCROOGE: Is it? Then go and buy it. *(Peter is convinced Scrooge is balmy.)* No... no, I'm serious. Here's the money. Get it and bring it back here. I'll give you a shilling for yourself. *(Peter starts out.)* Come back in five minutes and I'll give you half a crown. *(Peter dashes out. Scrooge laughs heartily.)* I'll send that turkey to Bob Cratchit's. He won't know who sent it. What a joke. Maybe I'll go there myself. No, that wouldn't do. I'll go to dinner with my nephew. He invited me. Of course he invited me. But I can't go looking like this. My whiskers. I've got to shave. *(Rushes around looking for a mirror and shaving things. The bells continue their tolling outside.)* Just listen to those bells. Makes me feel good just to hear them. *(Goes to the door)* Merry Christmas. Merry Christmas everybody. Certainly I'm talking to you. Mr... Mr... come in a minute. Come in. *(He leaves the door open and searches through a tin box in his desk. The man who yesterday solicited funds for the poor enters very hesitantly.)*

MAN: You wanted to see me?

SCROOGE: I did. Merry Christmas, sir. I'm sorry to say I didn't catch your name but I remember you. *(He shakes the man's limp hand.)* I hope you succeeded in collecting a great deal of money for the poor yesterday.

MAN: Well, I... I—

SCROOGE: My name is Scrooge. I fear it may not be very
pleasant to you. Allow me to ask your pardon. *(Handing over a
roll of money, he whispers in the man's ear.)* And will you have
the goodness?

MAN: *(Looking at the money)* Lord bless me. My dear Mr.
Scrooge, are you quite well this morning?

SCROOGE: Never felt better.

MAN: But this money... are you serious?

SCROOGE: If you please... not a farthing less. A great many back
payments are included in it, I assure you. A few for my partner,
Jacob Marley, too.

MAN: My dear sir, I don't know what to say.

SCROOGE: Don't say anything, please. Come and see me any
time you need help. Will you come and see me?

MAN: I will indeed. I will.

SCROOGE: Thank'ee. I'm much obliged to you. I thank you fifty
times. Bless you.

MAN: Bless you and Merry Christmas, sir.

(Scrooge lets him out the door.)

SCROOGE: Merry Christmas. *(Closes door)* Merry Christmas.
(Leaps in air) Whoops, it is a Merry Christmas! *(He starts to
shave.)* God rest you merry gentlemen. *(Holding shaving brush
thoughtfully)* God rest you merry gentlemen. Now what were the
rest of those words?

PETER: *(Knocking and bursting in)* Here you are sir... it's a
beauty... and here's your change.

SCROOGE: The change is for you, my good fellow, and another
half a crown for getting back so fast.

PETER: Thank you, Mr. Scrooge.

SCROOGE: You're a polite young man, you are. Now will you do me the favor of delivering this turkey? Let me see, I'd better write down the name and address on a piece of paper. *(Hunts for one and writes)* It's going to... Bob Cratchit.

PETER: Bob Cratchit!

SCROOGE: He's my clerk. Has a big family and I daresay they can use this turkey.

PETER: Yes, sir. I think they can.

SCROOGE: They live in Camden town. *(Hands paper to Peter)* Think you can find where they live?

PETER: I think so, sir.

SCROOGE: Delightful boy. By the way, how do you get to Camden town?

PETER: I'll walk.

SCROOGE: Walk? You can't carry that big bird all the way to Camden.

PETER: It won't feel heavy to me. I'll be thinking about how glad the family's going to be when they see it.

SCROOGE: Just the same, it's too far to walk. Here, get yourself a cab. No, wait... tell me. I've decided to go out to dinner. My nephew invited me. Insisted that I come. Yes, he did. Came all the way in here to ask me. I said I wouldn't go but I've changed my mind. How do I look?

PETER: Your coat needs a little brushing, sir. Here, let me.

SCROOGE: Thank'ee. Mighty kind of you to help an old man.

PETER: Glad to do it, sir. There, that's better.

SCROOGE: You think I look all right for Christmas dinner?

PETER: You look fine, sir.

SCROOGE: All right, then, run along. That bird ought to get in the oven.

PETER: Yes, sir. Merry Christmas, sir.

SCROOGE: Merry Christmas. Wait... you're not to say where that turkey came from... not a word. Promise?

PETER: But sir... I...
SCROOGE: I insist. Just say it came from a store.

PETER: They might think I stole it.

SCROOGE: You? Steal it? Nonsense. Well, tell them that the gentleman who sent it made you promise not to tell... promise?

PETER: If you wish, sir, I promise. Merry Christmas.

SCROOGE: Merry Christmas. *(The door closes. Scrooge goes on experimenting with the sound of the word.)* Merry Christmas, Merry Christmas.

(Lights go out on Scrooge singing a carol.)

ACT THREE
SCENE FOUR

(The carol is picked up off stage and when the lights come up on the Cratchit kitchen, the family is singing the carol and pulling their chairs around the stove.)

BOB: It's the finest Christmas we've ever had.

PETER: And the best dinner.

EDWARD: And there's a whole lot of turkey left too.

MRS. C: Peter, I'll never rest easy till you tell us where that turkey came from.
PETER: I'd tell you, Mother, but I promised I wouldn't...

EDWARD: You could whisper it to me.

PETER: You wouldn't want me to break a promise, would you?

BELINDA: Yes we would, tell us.

MRS. C: No, but I can't understand it, that's all.

PETER: Why don't you just accept it as a wonderful Christmas present?

MRS. C: I don't like accepting things without saying thank you.

PETER: I'll fill the cups.

BOB: Everybody think of a toast and then we'll put some chestnuts in the fire.

EDWARD: Goody. Chestnuts.

BOB: My, it does my heart good to see us all together like this. Sit closer to me, Tim.

EDWARD: I want to make the first toast.

BOB: Go on, Edward.

EDWARD: I make a toast to our turkey.

ALL: To the turkey.

BELINDA: I make a toast to whoever sent it.

ALL: To the sender.

PETER: I make a toast to the lady who cooked the turkey... to Mrs. Cratchit.

ALL: To Mrs. Cratchit.

MRS. C: *(Raising her glass)* A Merry Christmas to us all, my dears.

ALL: A Merry Christmas to us all.

BOB: And I will give you Mr. Scrooge, the founder of the feast.

MRS. C: Founder of the feast, indeed. I wish I had him here. I'd give him a piece of my mind to feast upon and I hope he'd have a good appetite for it.

BOB: My dear. Christmas.

MRS. C: When has he ever thought of Christmas?

BELINDA: Someone is coming up the steps.

MRS. C: Now, who could be coming to see us this afternoon? Answer the door, Peter.

(Peter crosses, opens the door, then closes it quickly.)

PETER: It's Mr. Scrooge!

ALL: Scrooge!

MRS. C: He's never set foot in this house before.

MARTHA: Then why does he have to choose today?

(Knocking on door)

BELINDA: He has no right to come here.

BOB: My dears. Somebody open the door.

PETER: Somebody else let him in. I'm going upstairs.

BOB: No, you'll stay right here. We'll do our best to welcome him.

(Peter hides behind a door. Mrs. C. and the girls stand haughtily. The children cling to Martha. Bob admits Scrooge.)

BOB: Mr. Scrooge.

SCROOGE: Merry Christmas, Bob.

BOB: Merry Christmas.

SCROOGE: You didn't expect to see me, did you?

BOB: Well, not exactly, sir. Will you come in?

SCROOGE: Thought I'd like to see what kind of a family you have.

BOB: Come in. *(Hesitates)* This is my wife, Mrs. Cratchit.

MRS. C: *(Stiffly)* How do you do?

SCROOGE: I'm honored, Mrs. Cratchit.

BOB: This is my daughter, Martha.

MARTHA: How do you do?

BOB: And this is my daughter, Belinda.

BELINDA: *(Equally cold)* How do you do?

BOB: And this Elizabeth... and Edward... and this is Tiny Tim.

SCROOGE: Ah, Tiny Tim.

(Tim gets up on his crutch and walks to Mr. Scrooge. He holds out his hand and Scrooge takes it.)

TIM: A Merry Christmas, Mr. Scrooge. We tried to sing you carols yesterday.

SCROOGE: Not you... surely not you. *(He's stunned.)*

TIM: Perhaps you'd like to hear some now.

SCROOGE: Thank you... thank you.

BOB: Wait. Where's Peter?

PETER: Here, Father.

BOB: Mr. Scrooge, this is my son, Peter.

PETER: How do you do, Mr. Scrooge.

SCROOGE: You... you...

PETER: Yes, sir, the same.

SCROOGE: But you didn't tell me—

PETER: I told you my name was Peter, sir. You didn't give me time to say Cratchit.

BOB: When did you see Mr. Scrooge, Peter?

PETER: This morning, Father.

SCROOGE: *(Dismayed)* Did you keep your promise?

PETER: I never break a promise, sir.

MRS. C: A promise!

(They all look at each other.)

PETER: Have a chair, Mr. Scrooge.

SCROOGE: No, thank you... no, thank you. I wouldn't interrupt a happy family party. I just wanted to say a word to Bob, here.

BOB: Yes, sir?

SCROOGE: I don't see how you support this family on your salary, Bob.

BOB: It's not easy, sir. But we're happy. *(Tim leans against him.)*

SCROOGE: I see. I see. But a little money wouldn't spoil your happiness, would it?

BOB: Well, sir, I don't know just what to say.

SCROOGE: Tomorrow you start work at a much higher salary.

ALL: Mr. Scrooge!

PETER: A toast to Mr. Scrooge! *(Thrusts a cup into Scrooge's hand)*

ALL: To Mr. Scrooge.

MRS. C: That turkey, Peter. Did... ?

PETER: Sh... I never break a promise.

MRS. C: *(Holding out her hand to Scrooge)* Mr. Scrooge, I beg your pardon. Please will you sit down and join our party?

TIM: Please, Mr. Scrooge.

(They put a chair for him and Tim sits near him.)

MRS. C: I want to make a toast. To Mr. Scrooge, the founder of the feast.

SCROOGE: The sweetest words I've ever heard...

BOB: A Merry Christmas to us all.

TIM: God bless us every one.

(All sing a carol as the curtain falls.)

CURTAIN

PROPERTY LIST

ACT ONE, SCENE 1. The Cratchit kitchen
      candle
      teapot
      china and silver for eight
      two blankets, crutch for Tiny Tim
      scarf hanging on wall or coat rack
      wood in wood box

SCENE 2. Scrooge's office
      shovel for Bob
      papers, pencil for Man
      crutch for Tim
      chain and bandage for Marley's Ghost
      watch, papers, pen, ink, toothpick on desk for Scrooge
      branch of holly for Ghost of Christmas Past
[Sound effects: tolling bell, murmur of ghostly voices, wind sounds]

ACT TWO, SCENE 1. Schoolroom
      book on table
      suitcases and caps for Fred, Rob, George

SCENE 2. Fezziwig's office
      watch for Fezziwig
      two lamps on desk for Dick
      fiddle for Fiddler
      holly wreath, scabbard for Ghost of Christmas Present
      broom, pot of porter for Scrooge

SCENE 3. The Cratchit kitchen
      Christmas packages for Martha
      roast goose
      pitcher of hot punch
      dish of potatoes
      potato masher
      large serving spoon
      bellows for fire
      wood for fire

ACT THREE, SCENE 1. Graveyard
      bundle of blankets for Charwoman
      bundle of shirts for Laundress
      pair of shoes, cuff links for Undertaker's Man

SCENE 2. The Cratchit kitchen
      Bible for Peter
      sewing for Mrs. Cratchit
      kettle, cup of tea for Belinda
      calling card for Bob

SCENE 3. Scrooge's office
      mirror, shaving set, soap, pencil, paper, tin box with bills
      and coins for Scrooge
      turkey in basket for Peter

NOTES